KHOKHLOMA
FOLK
PAINTING

KHOKHLOMA
FOLK
PAINTING

LENINGRAD
AURORA ART PUBLISHERS

Introduction, selection and notes by
TATYANA YEMELYANOVA

Photographs by
VLADIMIR STUKALOV

Designed by
GENNADY YABKEVICH

Translated from the Russian by
ROSEMARY SVETLICHNY

Х $\frac{80104-563}{023(01)-80}$ без объявления

4904000000

The northern part of the Gorky region is a single glorious expanse. A green carpet of water-meadows spreads along the lower left bank of the Volga and beyond them stretch boundless forests. In autumn these forests are particularly beautiful: dense fir-trees enhance the yellow-tinged lime and birch; the luxuriant maple canopies turn purple and orange and the sun tints the venerable oaks with noble bronze.

The golden foliage and lacy branches with scarlet clusters of ashberries recall the vibrant colours of Khokhloma — the folk painting which originated in these parts. Today this age-old art is flourishing anew. Aflame with gold and slender vermilion leaves, Khokhloma wooden tableware and furniture are world-famous. This remarkable Russian decorative craft dates from the seventeenth century and derives its name from the Volga mercantile village of Khokhloma, which has since become a major centre of folk art in the Soviet Union.

Equally old is the small town of Semionov, lying amidst forests and fields near the river Kerzhenets. Its wooden houses, built on a gently sloping hill, are noted for their finely carved window casings, ornate weather-vanes and chimneys. Thousands of tourists come to Semionov every year, wishing to know more about the folk art of the Gorky region. They visit the local handicrafts museum to see examples of masterly woodwork: carvings, sculptures, toys, Gorodets distaffs, gingerbread moulds and blocks for the hand-printing of fabrics. The main attraction of the museum, however, is its large collection of wooden Khokhloma ware.

On display are the gilded wooden bowls and dishes used daily in nineteenth century peasant households. Having dulled with age, they now glow softly in their showcases. But next to them shine the freshly varnished wares of a modern Semionov factory with their eye-catching floral designs. Today Khokhloma comes to Soviet people in a different form: magnificent dinner services adorn their tables on special occasions; ornamental vases and scoops lend poetry to modern décors; little caskets and spoons have become favourite souvenirs; painted beads, brooches and bracelets of wood add elegance to any fashion.

In the Khokhloma range of purely decorative objects, tableware takes pride of place. Besides the traditional bowls, spoons, small barrels and canisters, Khokhloma craftsmen produce superb kitchenware, including sets of dishes for fish soup, and vessels for jam, honey, and milk. These colourful vessels seem to radiate Russian hospitality.

Khokhloma ware is practical and makes an ideal ornament or gift. But it is also an original Russian folk art, a unique expression of national culture, and this too contributes to its growing fame. Today's craftsmen are reviving generations of experience in the art of turning, carving and painting wood.

Anyone who has seen these cups, canisters, small kegs and salt-cellars made of light, turned wood cannot fail to be impressed. Gracefully austere in form, yet rich in decoration, these modest articles are genuine works of art.

The motifs of Khokhloma painting are both simple and poetic, consisting of floral and plain geometrical patterns. Flowers and clusters of berries interwoven with sweeping grasses and golden tendrils curve gently over the wooden surfaces. Some of these compositions are restrained, others lavish; but all reflect the Russian people's love of nature and quest for beauty.

Khokhloma derives its bright, festive character from a distinctive matching of scarlet, black and gold. This dignified and lustrous combination gives the wooden dishes an aura of great value. That is all the more remarkable in that Khokhloma "gold" is not real, but the ingenious invention of Russian craftsmen.

To achieve the gold effect on wood is far from simple. First, the unpainted articles are primed and coated with drying oil. Next they are polished with powdered aluminium (powdered tin and more rarely silver were used in the past). The "silvered" wares are then painted with heat-resistant oil colours, varnished and fired in kilns. The heat turns the varnish yellow, the "silver" into "gold" and mellows the vivid design with an even, golden tone.

These "secret" techniques and traditions are today being maintained and developed by two large enterprises in the Gorky region. One is *Khokhlomskaya Rospis* in Semionov; the other is *Khokhlomskoi Khudozhnik*, which has branches in the Kovernino district villages of Siomino, Kuligino and Novopokrovskoye.

Between them, these famous enterprises employ about a thousand craftsmen (more accurately, crafts*women*), many of whom have received top awards for their skill. N. Denisova, O. Lushina, A. Tiukalov and A. Savinova have merited the title of Honoured Artist of the Russian Federation; and no fewer than eight craftswomen — A. Busova, O. Veselova, Ye. Dospalova, N. Ivanova, Z. Kiyova, O. Lushina, N. Salnikova and M. Siniova — won the Repin State Prize in January, 1970.

Their expertise has also earned them diplomas and medals at major Soviet and international exhibitions in Moscow, Paris, London, Brussels, Leipzig and Pyongyang.

The last decade in particular has seen exhibitions featuring the richest and most varied displays of modern Khokhloma painting. These include the Moscow exhibition *Contemporary Folk Art of the RSFSR* held in 1978; the 1975 Warsaw *Exhibition of Folk Art from the Socialist Countries*; the trade fairs in Berlin (1976) and Brno (1977); as well as *EXPO '67* in Montreal and *EXPO '70* in Osaka.

It has become an established custom at international exhibitions for the artists to demonstrate the painting technique itself; and this they do with consummate ease, entrancing onlookers with the sheer artistry of improvisation.

In Osaka's bustling exhibition village visitors queued for hours outside the Soviet pavilion to take away one of Yekaterina Dospalova's hand-painted souvenirs. Meanwhile the artist sat working at her low bench. Stroke by stroke she painted her designs, wild flowers and grasses flaming scarlet beneath her brush.

It was no accident that Khokhloma art emerged in the Volga region. These forested north-eastern parts of the Nizhni-Novgorod land once played a vital role in the economic and political life of Rus; their culture is as ancient as it is rich. Indeed, they inspired one of the greatest Russian folk poems, the legend of Kitezh — a town which was said to have vanished into lake Svetloyar during the Mongol invasion led by Khan Batu in 1238. This lake, which is pure and clear, lies hidden deep in the forest and its enigmatic beauty has lured wayfarers for centuries. But it was much later, in the early seventeenth century, that the region began to be populated in the true sense: large numbers of settlers came from all over Muscovy to seek refuge in the dense, impassable forests bordering the rivers Kerzhenets and Vetluga. Some of them were Old Believers who opposed the ecclesiastical reforms of the Patriarch Nikon; others were runaway serfs and rebellious *streltsi* (tsar's musketeers). These dissenters founded small, secluded monasteries in which were preserved treasures of ancient Russian art: icons, illuminated manuscripts, jewellery, precious fabrics and gold embroidery.

The sandy soil to the east of the Volga was scant and infertile. This obliged the newcomers to take up various handicrafts, of which woodwork — due to the abundance of timber in the area — was the most important. The peasant craftsmen would lavishly carve and paint almost everything they made: sleighs, shaft-bows, distaffs, battledores, looms and household utensils. They engraved intricate designs on gingerbread moulds and blocks for the hand-printing of fabrics and turned wood into lovely children's toys.

The Volga region boasted particularly elaborate carvings on the gables and gates of peasant cottages. These decorative panels depicted lush vegetation, legendary *Sirin* birds, water-sprites and lions with flowering stems for tails.

Craftsmen would often tint their carvings; most colourful of all, however, were the paintings on toys, boxes made of bast, Khokhloma ware and Gorodets distaffs.

Gorodets, once famed for its noisy bazaars, is a town on the Volga not far from Khokhloma. Yet the style of painting which developed there in the latter half of the nineteenth century differs markedly from Khokhloma art. Gorodets peasants specialized in painting distaffs. The broad *dontse* [1] was especially interesting with its lively illustrations of town and country life: brightly dressed couples, merry gatherings round tables laden with food and drink, or dashing horsemen and their proud steeds; such scenes were bordered with full-blown roses or vivid bouquets.

This peasant art is still admired for its bold pictorial style and rich, harmonious shades of blue, yellow, black and magenta. The everyday scenes of Gorodets painting indicate its fairly recent origins. The wide range of colours and the technique of painting without firing characteristic of Gorodets emphasize, by way of contrast, the unique qualities of Khokhloma, whose ornaments, sublime colouring and unusual technology were rooted in seventeenth century art and culture.

Khokhloma assumed a special place in the history of Volga-based handicrafts by virtue of its widespread production and sale, as well as the remarkable tenacity of the craft itself.

The Khokhloma method is thought to have arisen in the seventeenth century. At least, it is certain that by then the craftsmen of Nizhni-Novgorod were using powdered metals in decorating wooden tableware. We have proof that this was so on the estate of a certain boyar called Morozov, who wrote a letter to his bailiff in 1659 demanding to be sent "one hundred painted dishes polished with powdered tin, both large and medium, of the very same kind possessed by us earlier, not forgetting twenty large painted winebowls, twenty medium and twenty somewhat smaller..." [2] We are not told whether or not these vessels resembled gold.

By the seventeenth and eighteenth centuries wooden tableware was being made all over Rus. It was often coated with drying oil to make it harder and floral designs were painted on the rims of winebowls and scoops. But only the peasants of Nizhni-Novgorod knew the wonderful technique of imitating gold. It is more than likely that they were trying to copy precious ware turned from valuable types of wood; this was embellished with vermilion and real gold. It was made in monasteries, especially in the village of Klementyevo near Moscow. Klementyevo belonged to the lands of the Trinity — St Sergius Monastery, to which were added in the seventeenth century the eastern Volga villages of Khokhloma and Skorobogatovo.

The peasants from these villages volunteered to help in the monastery workshop where they could familiarize themselves with the production of fancy bowls and scoops. Thus it was the Khokhloma and Skorobogatovo areas which became the natural home of such precious-looking painted tableware.

But how did the peasants learn to give wood this golden sheen?

The older inhabitants to the east of the Volga recount a legend on this very subject: at the time of Tsar Alexis, there was a certain dissenter — an icon painter — who devised the art of making beautiful gilded bowls from wood. Although he lived clandestinely in the forests of Kerzhenets, his jealous rivals determined to capture him and even the palace guard "strode forth into the lands of Semionov" with the aim of bringing him back to Moscow. On hearing of their approach, however, the fugitive craftsman summoned all the people from the neighbouring villages, told them his secret, gave out brushes and paints and then set light to his house, where he was burned alive. The sparks of this fire are said to have "kindled the fame of Khokhloma colours throughout the forest villages and settlements". [3]

This legend supports the assumption held by modern researchers that Khokhloma technology evolved under the influence of icon painting which thrived in the monasteries of Old Believers. Seventeenth century craftsmen in Nizhni-Novgorod were accustomed to working with gold in a variety of ways. Quite often they would use silver powder to "gild" the background of icons. The powder was coated with drying oil of an amber colour achieved by adding to the oil alder and rowan bark. The surface was probably then exposed to high temperatures in a kiln.

This technique, not unlike Khokhloma, was also used for ornamentation. In the Gorky Art Museum there are seventeenth century icon cases whose painted designs recall precious oriental textiles with luxuriant branches covered in fabulous golden flowers and fantastic leaves glittering against red or green backgrounds (*plates 1, 5*).

The roots of Khokhloma can be traced back to Old Russian ornamental art, as there is an obvious link between Khokhloma designs and the floral decorations on icons, frescoes, manuscripts, seventeenth century utensils, cloths and gold embroidery. Although peasant art came under various influences, it modified these to create its own distinct style, largely dictated by the need for cheap and durable tableware.

The oldest surviving tableware dates from the late eighteenth and early nineteenth centuries. Typical of this period are winebowls, large drinking vessels passed around at a banquet for everyone to drink from in turn, strong and beautifully shaped, as well as mugs and huge dishes. These vessels were only partially gilded in strips on a black or vermilion background. Sometimes the designs were executed with thick brush-strokes, but usually the craftsmen employed stencils similar to those for hand-printing cloth. It is hardly surprising that Khokhloma artists adopted the designs and compositions used in textile printing, as this was a common industry in the Semionov and Vetluga districts. Each utensil had its own motif, such as the tiny silver flowers on curving stems which decorated mugs; the little trails of gold and silver stars, golden red pomegranates and fan-shaped shrubs running over winebowls, and the rosette arrangements of silver bead-like dots in the centre of cups (*plate 6*).

It was bowls of this type which the court physician, G. Rehmann, noticed while visiting Makaryev fair, the largest in Russia, in 1805. The fair used to skirt the walls of Makaryev Monastery, whose golden cupolas overlook the confluence of the rivers Kerzhenets and Volga. Here, in this colourful market-town, with its cosmopolitan bustle and countless stalls, selling everything from Persian carpets and Kashmir shawls to Siberian furs and nielloed silver from Ustiug, Rehmann was struck by "a long row of carts bearing wooden vessels of everyday use, many of which may be considered rarities of their kind." Rehmann was referring to the dishes and bowls turned from lime-wood in which Russian peasants served their food. He continues: "Among many other objects worthy of curiosity, I was often astonished by the great bowls of as much as one and a half *arsheen* [equal to 107 centimetres] in diameter turned from wood, which did not show the least signs of cracking, in spite of the scorching heat and the strong reflection of the sun's rays from the sand where they lay. There were smaller bowls than these with lids, which held up to forty smaller ones placed one inside the other... Almost all the vessels made for special occasions are coated with yellow and dark varnish and adorned on the outside with silver and gold. These [he concludes] are veritable examples of the art of turning."[4] He even mentions where the vessels were made—the villages of the Semionov district.

The scholar and geographer, E. Ziablovsky, also visited this district at the beginning of the last century, commenting on wares made by the villagers of Nikolskoye: "Their wares are light, clean and durable, and the yellow and black varnish on them is most hard and clear, being prepared from boiled linseed oil."[5]

Vast forests and the proximity of trading routes assisted the growth of the craft. By the mid-nineteenth century the principles of Khokhloma technology had been laid down; the characteristic designs and compositional patterns were established.

Khokhloma follows various principles, depending on the type, size and function of the article to be decorated. The cheapest bowls — which could be seen in every peasant home — bore very simple designs. The craftsman would take a stencil made of felt, a dried puff-ball or a porous sponge and dip it in paint. On the surface of the bowl he would then paint black and red lozenges, stars and spirals. Alternating on a plain gold background, they produced a beautiful rhythmical effect. Sometimes they were combined with light brush-strokes — either applied randomly along the rim of the bowl or arranged like a flower in the bottom. Even these primitive compositions reflected the village craftsman's sensitivity to his art, his ability to decorate a surface without impairing the effect of the gold background. His tools were humble, but with them he created the most attractive designs (*plate 8*).

The *travny* or grass design was painted on larger or more sophisticated articles. With rapid, tense brush-strokes the craftsman depicted blades of grass or feathery leaves. This light, delicate design highlighted the beautiful proportions of gold dishes, kegs and wooden mats.

The huge *artel* bowls measuring up to one and a half *arsheen* in diameter are particularly interesting. These were made to contain enough helpings for an entire team of workmen and sometimes they bore inscriptions like "This bowl is for barge haulers for them to eat their fill. Our master we shall serve as we sing our song."

Often craftsmen would decorate the bottoms of these bowls with rosettes consisting of blades of grass radiating outwards from the centre. This design was popularly known as *ryzhik*, meaning "the red one", because of its resemblance to either the reddish wild mushroom of the same name or to the sun, called *Ryzhy* (red) *Yarilo* after the ancient pagan sun god. The rosette was often enclosed within a lozenge, in which case it became a *prianik*, or gingerbread design. The sides of the bowls are decorated with wreathes of foliage so luxuriant that they even seem to be growing: it is as if the branches are putting out their curling tendrils with clusters of berries one after another. This prolific motif is best suited to a spherical surface where repetition acquires clarity and harmony (*plate 18*).

11

In another instance the composition was based on the principle of contrast: the *prianik*-rosette was enlarged and a series of curving dabs were painted along the rim like the feathers of a fairy-tale bird. Applied in a brisk manner, they produced a rapid circular rhythm and made a striking contrast with the static *prianik*-rosette (*plate 15*).

Khokhloma art reverently preserved the ancient *travny* or grass motif. But it also made bold and unexpected changes such as the wavy sprigs adorning bowls, the leafy shrubs on stout little kegs and salt-cellars, the exquisite sedge on slim canisters and the spiralling tendrils on their lids.

The peasant artist had a boundless imagination, for he never painted any two designs exactly alike; each new version displayed his remarkable capacity to improvise, to dispense with preliminary sketches. This accounts for the expressiveness of the *verkhovoye* technique used for painting grass designs: fluid brush-strokes representing blades of grass were applied in silhouette on a gold ground. The rhythm of the pattern depended on how the artist used his brush; whether the motion was bold and energetic or smooth and relaxed it always showed confidence and precision (*plates 4, 9, 17*).

It took generations of artists to develop this style, which combines proven techniques with spontaneity and apparent simplicity. Every brush-stroke, be it heavy or light, obeys a certain law; while alluding to nothing more than a shape, it instantly evokes the vivid impression of a flourishing plant.

The fiery splashes of vermilion reflect the generous Russian soul, a lively attachment to nature, the peasant's dream of beauty and his desire to turn an ordinary plant into an exotic one with fanciful tendrils. We are reminded of the imagery of country wedding songs, in which the "golden hop" twines, "azure flowers" bloom and "silken grasses" bow down to the bride and groom.

Although the grass theme was the peasant's favourite, he often gave preference to the *pod listok* composition of simple leaves on branches (occasionally complemented by grasses) and the *drevko* design — a stylized tree with big flowers and leaves and curling tendrils.

Verkhovoye painting is related to the tradition of "spontaneous painting" which was popular in the Volga region in the seventeenth and eighteenth centuries. *Fonovoye* painting emerged in the mid-nineteenth century and cultivated different, more involved principles and techniques: the artist traced the outline of the design thinly in black. He then coloured in the background, bringing the remaining silvery design to life with light brushwork and hatching. After the utensil had been varnished and fired in a kiln, the golden flowers and leaves came alive against a bright red or deep black background. This was the method of painting the "curly" or *kudrina* design, consisting of golden tendrils. If painted in series, like the crests of waves, they made an attractive gold border. Craftsmen were very fond of decorating the rims of bowls and canisters in this way. The *kudrina* motif often appears as a branch with fleshy leaves, reminiscent of the foliage patterns carved on peasant cottages. As one elderly artist, N. Podogov, tells us, craftsmen modified these patterns to suit the curved surfaces of Khokhloma ware, rounding the leaf outlines accordingly (*plates 10, 12*). *Kudrina* was liked for the generalization of form and the vibrance of its gold patches. It adorned small basins and spoons, yet was most effective on very large objects such as round stools, bowls and shaft-bows.

One can see similar designs on shaft-bows dating from the mid-nineteenth century. They are very much like the illuminations of ancient manuscript books: the branches with curling leaves are finer and are clasped with rings. Such drawings obviously influenced the *kudrina* motif and may even have determined its technique: instead of thick brush-strokes conveying succulent grasses, the *kudrina* motif is based on contours, gold patches and meticulous hatching.

However, the somewhat laborious *fonovoye* painting was evidently confined to objects which were either commissioned or intended as gifts and few of these have survived. They often bore signatures or inscriptions such as "This shaft-bow belongs to the peasant, Simeon Ivanov Grishin, village of Retkino, 1855."

The *verkhovoye* technique of painting on a gold ground was simple and succinct. For this reason it persisted as the main method of decorating vessels sold in bulk, that is, in batches of a thousand.

By the second half of the nineteenth century Khokhloma production had expanded considerably, having spread to the provinces of Kostroma and even Viatka. Nevertheless, Khokhloma in the Semionov district continued to be its centre. "There is remarkable activity in the Khokhloma area," wrote the *Nizhni-Novgorod Provincial News* in 1855. "One village makes wooden blocks, from which another turns bowls, while, a third village paints them." This shows the unique division of labour which had evolved by the mid-nineteenth century. There were over five hundred turner's workshops in the Semionov district alone.

Workshops were set up on the narrow, but fast-flowing rivers Kerzhenets, Linda and Uzol. The water drove a wheel which in turn rotated logs studded with wooden blocks; using various chisels, turners would dexterously cut and round these blocks. Horse-driven lathes and lathes worked by hand also existed.

The turned articles were then taken to the village of Khokhloma where they were bought by peasant dyers. These craftsmen lived in tidy, close-knit villages and their premises were unmistakable: a dye-house smelled strongly of paint and burned drying oil and its entrance was always cluttered with baskets containing the finished wares. A wealthier peasant would own a larger dye-house equipped with two enormous kilns, numerous drying shelves and a spacious cellar. There was room for ten people to work: men would paint their articles while women and children performed auxiliary tasks such as priming and coating the wares with drying oil. Spoons, however, were usually painted by women and girls.

In all, they produced up to forty types of spoons of various shapes and colours made of birch, maple and even palm trees brought from the Caspian. With their adroit and delicate hands, the girls of Semionov adorned their spoons with flowers, birds, houses, and pretty noblewomen, painted either in ink or size prepared from red lead or chrome yellow; their "monastery" spoons bore other motifs: bell-towers, torrets and small towns. The "golden" spoons of Khokhloma were stencilled with tiny stars or adorned with the more elaborate *pod listok* and *kudrina* designs. The dyer usually packed these beautiful spoons into the baskets last of all, so as to show off his wares to their best advantage.

Spoon-makers dwelled in separate settlements. During fine summer weather they would often work in the open, outside their cottages. First, they hewed the wooden blocks with an axe; then they made the hollow of the spoon by gouging out the extraneous wood. Finally came the handle, which they rounded off at the end and grooved. One observer, A. Lemann, expressed amazement at their knack of using a "rude axe" to transform a piece of birch-wood into the daintiest mustard spoon in a mere fifteen minutes. He was so struck by the spoon-makers' enthusiasm for their craft that he wrote: "Outside almost every cottage was a tree-stump where sat a spoon-maker, hollowing spoons. Around him lay a mass of white shavings, proving that work had begun before sunrise." [6]

By the 1880s there were twenty thousand artists engaged in spoon production near Semionov and thirty-five million spoons were despatched for sale every day.

NOTES

[1] The Russian distaff was composed of two elements: the *lopastka*, or blade, a vertical board with a broad flat upper part on which the bunch of flax was fixed, and the *dontse*, or base, a horizontal board on which the spinner sat. After the work was finished, the *dontse* was hung, as a rule, on the wall next to the icons and embroidered cloth (which always had the "place of honour" in peasant huts).

[2] *Акты хозяйства боярина Морозова*, т. 2, М.—Л., 1945, с. 92 (*Housekeeping Journal of the Boyar Morozov*, v. 2, Moscow — Leningrad, 1945, p. 92).

[3] *Нижегородские предания и легенды*, Горький, 1971, с. 117—119 (*Legends of Nizhni-Novgorod*, Gorky, 1971, pp. 117—119).

[4] Г. Реман, «Макарьевская ярмарка», *Северный архив*, 1822, № 9, с. 201—202 (G. Rehmann, "Makaryev Fair", *Northern Archives*, 1822, No 9, pp. 201—202).

[5] Е. Зябловский, *Землеописание Российской империи для всех состояний*, 4, СПб., 1810, с. 154 (E. Ziablovsky, *Geography of the Russian Empire for All Statuses*, 4, St Petersburg, 1810, p. 154).

[6] А. Леман, «Ложка и ложкари. Впечатления и заметки», *Исторический вестник*, 1902, № 6, с. 911 (A. Lemann, "Spoons and Spoon-makers: Impressions and Notes", *Historical Bulletin*, 1902, No 6, p. 911).

[7] Е. Медиокритский, «Крашение посуды и мебели в Скоробогатовской волости Макарьевского уезда», в кн.: *Труды комиссии по исследованию кустарной промышленности в России*, вып. 9, Спб., 1883, с. 2186 (E. Mediokritsky, "The Decoration of Tableware and Furniture in the Skorobogatovo District of Makaryev", in: *The Findings of the Research Commission on Handicraft Production in Russia*, 9, St Petersburg, 1883, p. 2186).

Plates

1
Icon case. Late 17th century

2
Plate. Mid-19th century
Grass design

3
Vessel for soaking flax. Early 20th century
"Plaited" design, by Osip Lavrentyev

4
Barrel. Early 20th century
Grass design

5
Icon case (detail).
Late 17th century

6
Bowl. Late 18th or early 19th century
Stencilled design

7
Winebowl. First half
of 19th century
Stencilled design

8
Cups. Mid-19th century
Design on a gold ground
(*verkhovoye* painting)

9

Cup. Second half of 19th century
Grass design

10

Cup. Early 20th century
Kudrina and "plaited" designs

11 →

Cups. Early 20th century
Gold pattern on a coloured ground (*fonovoye* painting), "plaited" design

12 →

Scoops. Second half of 19th century
Grass and *kudrina* designs

13 ←
Dish (detail). Early 20th century
"Plaited" design

14
Goblet. Late 19th century
Grass design

15
Dish. Mid-19th century
Osochka ("sedge") and *prianik* designs

16
Decorative plate. 1900
Drevko design, by Prokofy Raspopin

17
Goblet. Second half of 19th century
Grass design

18
Dish (detail). Mid-19th century
Grass and *prianik* designs

19
Duck-shaped salt-cellar. Early
20th century
Ornamentation on a gold ground
(*verkhovoye* painting)

20, 21
Shaft-bow (detail). Second half of 19th century
Gold pattern on a coloured ground (*fonovoye* painting)

22
Canisters. 1950s
Gold pattern on a coloured ground (*fonovoye* painting), by Alexander Muravyov

23
Decorative plate. 1920s
Kudrina design, by Georgi Matveyev

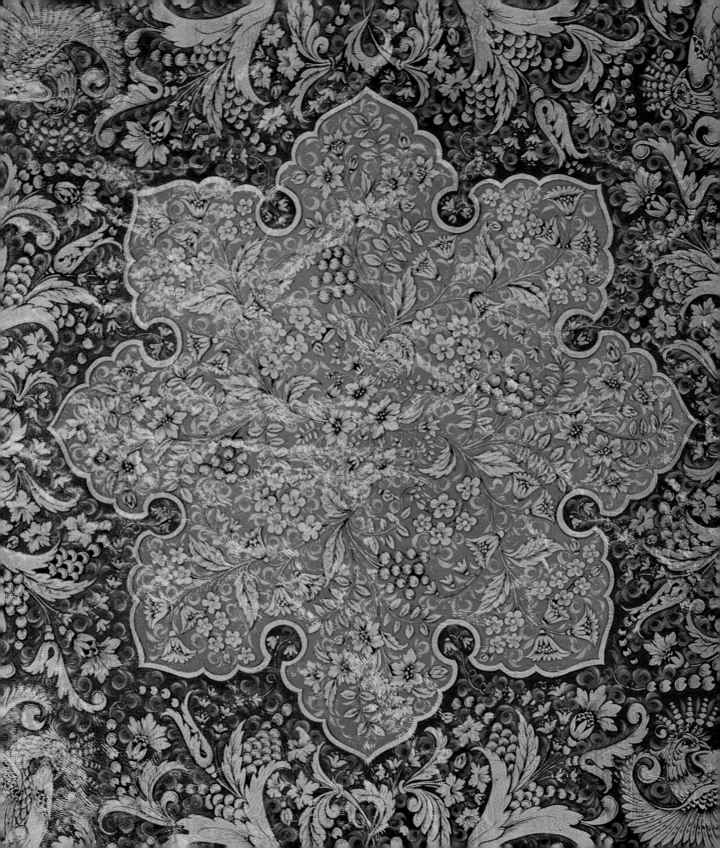

24
Table-top (detail). 1948
Gold pattern on a coloured
ground (*fonovoye* painting),
by Alexander Muravyov

25

Stool (detail). 1937
Grass design

26
Duck-shaped scoop with
miniature scoops. 1940s
Gold pattern on a coloured
ground (*fonovoye* painting),
by Yelena Sennikova

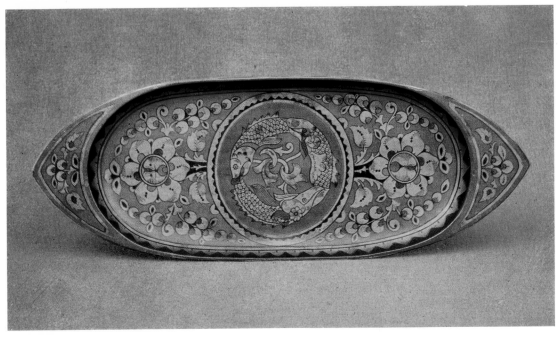

33
Tray. 1950
Kudrina design

34
Tray. 1936
Kudrina design, by Stepan Krasilnikov

35
Dish. 1935
Grass design, by Fiodor Bedin

36
Dish, "Fishes". 1930s
Gold pattern on a coloured ground
(*fonovoye* painting), by Ivan Smirnov

37
Vase. 1930s
Grass design, by Ivan Smirnov

38
Duck-shaped scoop. 1943
Gold pattern on a coloured ground
(*fonovoye* painting), by Natalya
Chikalova-Denisova

39
Canisters. 1940s
Gold pattern on a coloured ground
(*fonovoye* painting), by Maria Rodionova
and Alexandra Savinova

40 →
Table-top (detail). 1946
Gold pattern on a coloured ground
(*fonovoye* painting), by Nina Ivanova

41
Decorative plate. 1940s
Gold pattern on a coloured ground (*fonovoye*
painting), by Zinaida Vorobyeva

42
Vase. 1938
Gold pattern on a coloured
ground (*fonovoye* painting),
by Maria Kuznetsova

43
Cockerel-shaped scoop. 1959
Design on a gold ground (*verkhovoye*
painting), by Olga Bulganina

44
Dish, "Wild Strawberries". 1959
Design on a gold ground (*verkhovoye*
painting), by Olga Bulganina

Goblet and box. 1950s
Gold pattern on a coloured ground
(*fonovoye* painting), by Nikolai Podogov

Scoop. 1950s
Gold pattern on a coloured ground
(*fonovoye* painting), by Nikolai Podogov

47
Coffee set. 1972
Gold pattern on a coloured ground
(*fonovoye* painting), by Nina Morozova

48
Table-top (detail). 1950s
Gold pattern on a coloured
ground (*fonovoye* paint-
ing), by Nikolai Podogov

49
Canister. 1959
Kudrina design, by Olga
Bulganina

50
Tableware. 1977
Kudrina design, by Yekaterina
Dospalova and Galina Volkova

51
Small tub. 1973
Grass design, by Yekaterina Dospalova
and Maria Gladkova

52
Decorative panel (detail). 1960s
Grass design, by Stepan Veselov

53
Decorative panel, "Birds". 1969
Kudrina design, by Nina Ivanova

58
Vase. 1967
Kudrina design

59
Decorative panel. 1967
Kudrina design, by Marfa Siniova

65 ←

Plates, "Cockerel". 1977
Design on a gold ground (*verkhovoye*
painting), by Stepan Veselov

66

Honey set. 1977
Gold pattern on a coloured
ground (*fonovoye* painting),
by Liubov Poliashova

67
Decorative panel, "Firebird". 1970
Kudrina design, by Nina Ivanova

Jam set. 1975
Gold pattern on a coloured ground
(*fonovoye* painting), by Yekaterina
Dospalova and Nina Morozova

69
Beer set. 1970
Design on a gold ground
(*verkhovoye* painting), by Nina
Ivanova and Nina Salnikova

70
Duck-shaped scoop with miniature
scoops. 1970
Gold pattern on a coloured ground
(*fonovoye* painting), by Maria Zasovkina

71
Soup set. 1971
Gold pattern on a coloured ground
(*fonovoye* painting), by Nina Morozova,
Alexandra Savinova, Nina Salnikova
and Nina Ivanova

72
Cup, "Leaves". 1968
Design on a gold ground
(*verkhovoye* painting),
by Olga Lushina

73
Canister. 1967
Design on a gold ground
(*verkhovoye* painting),
by Nina Salnikova

74
Wine set. 1976
Kudrina design, by Nina Ivanova

75
Canisters. 1970
Kudrina design,
by Valentina Grachova

76
Decorative plate. 1974
Gold pattern on a coloured ground
(*fonovoye* painting), by Nina Ivanova

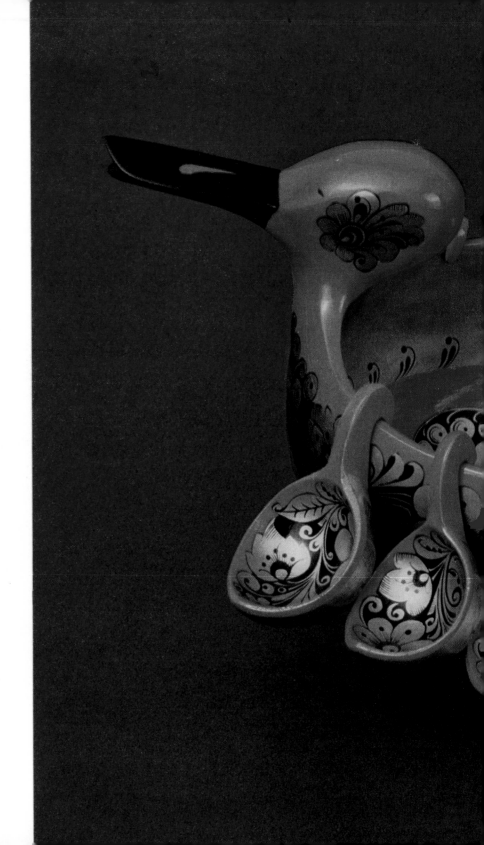

77
Duck-shaped scoop with miniature
scoops. 1968
Kudrina design, by Galina
Volkova and Mikhail Uglanov

78
Mead set. 1970
Gold pattern on a coloured ground
(*fonovoye* painting), by Ivan Sorokin

79
Canister. 1971
Gold pattern on a coloured ground
(*fonovoye* painting), by Tatyana Melnikova

80
Table-top. 1976
Gold pattern on a coloured ground
(*fonovoye* painting)

81
Honey set. 1970
Gold pattern on a coloured ground
(*fonovoye* painting), by Yekaterina
Dospalova and Faina Yuzikova

82
Vase. 1969
Gold pattern on a coloured
ground (*fonovoye* painting),
by Maria Savelyeva

83
Kvass set. 1970
Gold pattern on a coloured
ground (*fonovoye* painting),
by Ivan Sorokin and
Marfa Siniova

89
Spoons. 1970s
Gold pattern on a coloured ground
(*fonovoye* painting); ornamentation
on a gold ground (*verkhovoye* painting); *kudrina* design

90
Table-top. 1971
Gold pattern on a coloured ground
(*fonovoye* painting), by Nina Ivanova

91
Cup, "Autumn Leaves". 1977
Design on a gold ground (*verkhovoye*
painting), by Galina Volkova

92 ←
Set for fish soup. 1968
Gold pattern on a coloured ground
(*fonovoye* painting), by Yekaterina
Dospalova, Nina Morozova and
Alexandra Savinova

93

Canisters. 1969
Kudrina design, by Ivan Sorokin

94

Compote set. 1960s
Drevko design, by Marfa Siniova

95 →
Small barrels. 1975
Gold pattern on a coloured ground
(*fonovoye* painting)

96
Flour scoops. 1971
Gold pattern on a coloured ground
(*fonovoye* painting)

97
Cup. 1973
Gold pattern on a coloured ground
(*fonovoye* painting), by Alexandra Busova

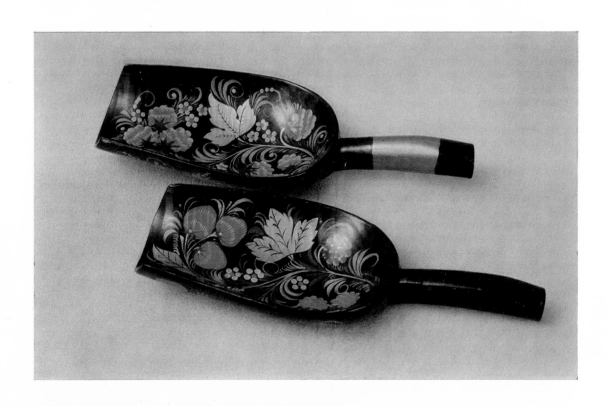

98
Tray, "Red Whortleberries". 1970
Gold pattern on a coloured ground
(*fonovoye* painting), by Marfa Siniova

99
Dinner service. 1973
Kudrina design, by Nina Ivanova

100
Kvass set. 1969
Kudrina design, by Nina Ivanova
and Ivan Sorokin

Tableware. 1974
Grass design, by Yekaterina Serova

Beads and belts. 1970
Grass and *kudrina* designs

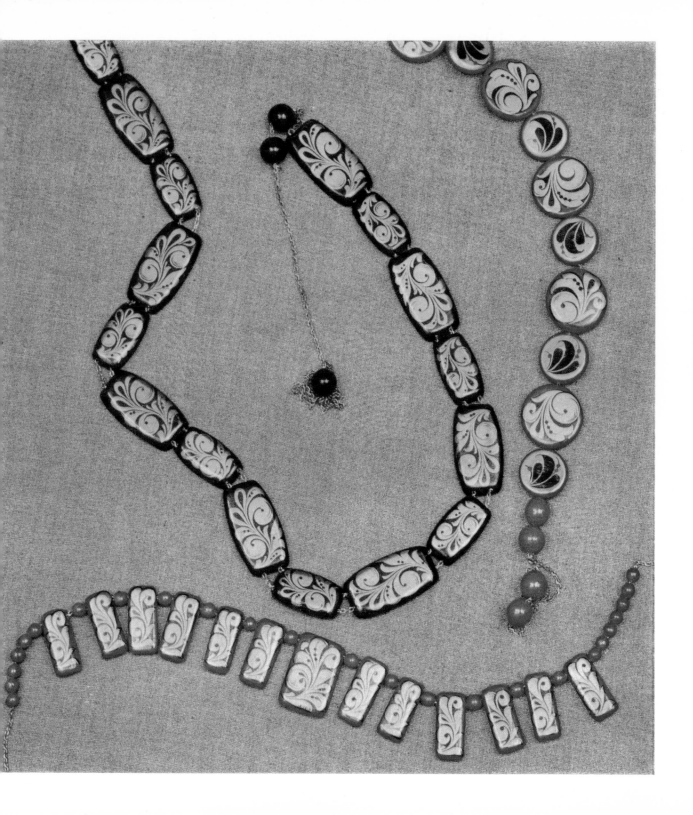

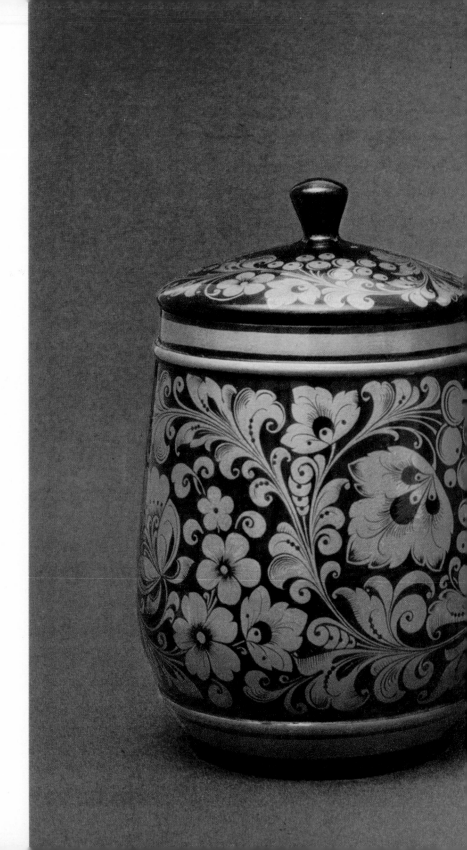

103 ←

Mug and tray. 1970
Gold pattern on a coloured ground
(*fonovoye* painting), by Marfa
Siniova and Ivan Sorokin

104 ←

Sketch. 1960
Kudrina design, by Antonina
Kuznetsova

105

Compote set. 1969
Kudrina design, by Nina Ivanova

106
Decorative panel. 1976
Grass design, by Olga Lushina

107
Decorative panel. 1960s
Osochka and *prianik* designs
by Stepan Veselov

108
Honey set. 1970
Gold pattern on a coloured ground
(*fonovoye* painting), by Yekaterina
Dospalova and Nina Morozova

109 →
Dinner service. 1960s
Kudrina design, by Natalya Denisova

110 →
Spoons. 1970s
Gold pattern on a coloured ground
(*fonovoye* painting); ornamentation
on a gold ground (*verkhovoye* painting); *kudrina* design

111
Autumn (detail). 1937
Painted decoration, by Ivan Tiukalov and
Yakov Krasilnikov

LOCATION OF THE ITEMS REPRODUCED IN THE PRESENT VOLUME

Arts and Crafts Museum, Semionov,
*15, 16, 17, 18, 22, 23, 24, 26, 27, 34, 36, 37,
38, 39, 40, 41, 42, 48, 59, 69, 73, 75, 79, 93*

Khokhlomskaya Rospis Factory, Semionov,
*50, 51, 56, 58, 60, 61, 63, 70, 71, 74, 81, 82,
91, 92, 94, 95, 102, 103*

Museum of History and Architecture, Gorky,
3, 20, 21, 30, 45, 46

Art Museum, Gorky, *1, 5, 43, 44, 49, 62, 78, 83*

Ethnographic Museum, Leningrad,
2, 6, 7, 8, 9, 10, 11, 12, 19, 28, 33

Russian Museum, Leningrad, *4, 13, 14*

Museum of History and Arts, Zagorsk,
25, 29, 31, 32, 35, 111

Private collection, Gorky, *52, 72, 107*

Private collection, Semionov, *104*

P. Zotova collection, Leningrad, *47, 53, 55,
57, 64, 67, 68, 76, 77, 84, 90, 98, 99, 100, 105,
108, 109, 110*

Private collections, Leningrad, *54, 65, 66,
80, 85, 86, 87, 88, 89, 96, 97, 101, 106*

ХОХЛОМА

Альбом (на английском языке)
Издательство «Аврора». Ленинград. 1980. Изд. № 2270. (7-10)
Printed and bound in the USSR